Ask...

--- ✳ ---

How to Get
What You Want and
Need at Work

Ask...

How to Get

What You Want and

Need at Work

PRISCILLA H. CLAMAN

Insights

BOSTON

Published by Insights Incorporated, Boston

Copyright © 2002 by Priscilla H. Claman

All rights reserved

Printed in the United States of America

First Edition, 2002

First Printing, 2002

Ask... : how to get what you want and need at work / Priscilla H. Claman. ____ 1st American ed. 120 p.

ISBN 0-939532-~~00-X~~ 02-6

1. Claman, Priscilla H. 2. Careers 3. Human Resources 4. Management

Copies are available from Insights at 800-323-6809

and from Career Strategies Incorporated at 617-227-5517 or

www.career-strategies.com

❋ Contents ❋

✳ Acknowledgements ✳

My thanks to my colleagues in human resources, to the many excellent managers I have worked with, and especially to my clients for the ideas and approach presented here. It is my hope that their experiences will help others achieve success and satisfaction at work. The fact that these ideas exist in book form is due to the optimism and persistence of Heather Peck and the continuing, loving support of my husband, Victor.

You Should Read this Book if You Want to Be Successful at Work

You've probably experienced it—that rush of energy that comes when you are happy and satisfied at work. It almost doesn't feel like work. The day goes by quickly. You may feel tired, but you are proud of what you have been able to accomplish. It seems easy for you to be successful. When you and your work are well matched, it can energize your whole life.

The opposite is also true. You may have experienced that as well. It's that feeling of being drained and exhausted before you've even had a chance to put in the effort. It's like an undertow that can undermine your best intentions. You can't figure out why things are going wrong, and you don't have any idea what to do about it.

For many of us, it is fate or luck or maybe our manager that seems to make the difference between work that energizes us and work that drains us. This may have been true in the past, but it's not true any longer. It is you who can make the biggest difference in your work life.

In the world of hierarchical organizations and one-company careers of the '60s and '70s, your boss chose your next assignment for you. Your company had a career path for you to follow. You didn't ask for yourself; you did what you were told to do. Sometimes your assignments were great; sometimes they were painful. But, in return for doing what you were told to do, you had a career for life. That was the unwritten deal.

Now that companies grow, die, merge, change hands over and over again, and managers come and go in less than a year, it has become our own responsibility to manage our careers—to make sure we are happy and satisfied at work. But we continue to be stuck in patterns that inhibit career effectiveness. We have been carefully trained not to call attention to ourselves, to boast, or to ask for what we need. We have picked Cinderella and the Lone Ranger as role models.

Cinderella worked hard, did her best, and suffered without complaining—all in the expectation that some powerful person would come along some time, notice her, and provide her with the respect and position she deserved.

The real Cinderella was lucky. For the rest of the Cinderellas out there, that kind of recognition is rare. After a while, when the recognition and the rewards don't come, resentment sets in. "Why doesn't the executive vice president even acknowledge the extra work it took me to put that report together?"

The answer may be that the executive vice president had no idea how much work went into completing the report, or even that Cinderella did it. For most Cinderellas, speaking up and asking for a raise or another assignment after completing a major assignment seems impossible to do. It's easier to think, "The executive vice president should have known, if she only cared…"

The Lone Ranger is also anonymous. He rides into town wearing a mask, solves the problem at some personal risk, and rides out again, refusing to accept the adulation of the townspeople. He never talks about himself or asks for help. He operates as a real loner, not as a member of a community with real expectations for himself and others.

Like Cinderella's pattern of waiting to be discovered, the Lone Ranger's pattern of going it alone is a guarantee of frustration in this new career world. If you are a Cinderella or a Lone Ranger, you are not alone. Men and women, computer programmers and marketing officers—all kinds of people have trouble asking for themselves. Whether it is because of their childhoods, their professional training, or their personal preferences, not asking can be a strong behavior pattern.

Changing deep, ingrained patterns of behavior isn't easy. This book asks you to change a pattern of behavior that may be a deep part of you. Asking for what you need at work may feel like a big risk the first time you do it. This book will give you all kinds of ways to reduce the risk you feel and increase your chances of success. But, like all changes in behavior, practice will make those changes easier.

Also, like all changes in behavior, thinking about what you will gain from this change helps your motivation. Remember the times when your work seemed easy, when it filled you with strength and confidence?

Everyone deserves to have that feeling of success and satisfaction at work. You do, too. And you are much more likely to have that wonderful feeling if you learn to ask.

Asking is the one critical skill that everyone must learn to manage a career in this time of uncertainty and change. Pick any section in this book, any story that appeals to you. They are all true stories, although their names and some of the facts may be changed. Then try out asking yourself. You'll be happy you did.

— *Priscilla H. Claman*

❋ Introduction ❋

Why People Don't Ask

Most people spend their daylight hours at work. For hours and hours, years and years, they spend their energy and intelligence striving to earn a living. And yet, even when they succeed, most people are not satisfied. Success isn't enough if success only means making a lot of money and having a job others envy.

"I've worked hard to get to where I am. But now, my heart's not in it. I'm not learning and growing. I'm bored. There must be a better job for me."

Who told me that? The thirty-five-year-old software engineer? The twenty-five-year-old phone-based customer service representative? The forty-five-year-old partner in a law firm? The fifty-five-year-old executive? In truth, they all told me that or something like it.

Just when Americans have become more successful in career and financial terms, they have become ever more dissatisfied in their careers.

After working with thousands of people in hundreds of different kinds of jobs, and with employers including banks, high tech firms, biotech companies, financial services firms, universities, insurance companies, and consulting firms, I have come to a simple conclusion:

> ***Most people don't take the initiative
> to make themselves happy at work
> —they don't ask.***

They don't ask for the assignments they want, for the salary increase they deserve, or for the opportunities to learn or make greater contributions. They don't ask when they don't understand something. They don't ask when they need help. And they don't know how to ask so that they get what they ask for.

This is a book about how to ask for what you want to make yourself more satisfied at work. There are no easy fixes. Work is not supposed to be easy. But if you make a habit of assessing yourself and what you want, and then asking for it, you will have a much greater chance to feel the energy that comes from doing the work you enjoy.

This is not a book about Machiavellian office politics. To be good at that you have to be able to believe what you don't really believe. Very few people can do that. Besides, faking it is too exhausting over time. This book is for those who don't want to be political, who wouldn't know how, and who want to be more authentically themselves at work.

But before we get started, let's first have a look at why people don't ask. I believe it comes down to three things that people believe.

1. "People Might Say No."

It's true, people might say no. Or they might even get angry and say no. Sometimes, asking makes you feel like the person you were in high school asking for a prom date. You might get rejected. But, if you don't ask, you probably won't get to the prom.

As the saying goes, If you always do what you've always done, you'll always get what you've always gotten. Is that enough?

Consultant:

A thirty-five-year-old consultant came to me to change either his company or his career. He loved his colleagues. His work was great. He just couldn't handle the travel anymore. Besides, his wife was pregnant with twins. He had to spend more time at home. I asked him, "If your current job included less travel, would you be happy? Have you ever thought of asking for little or no travel?"

"Oh, I couldn't ask for that. Everyone has to travel at my firm. They wouldn't understand. They'd get angry with me. It would be much easier to find another job somewhere else." It took a little thought and planning to make it work, but he asked for his job without the travel and got everything he wanted, plus a promotion.

It's common for people to fear that people will get angry. It is rare, but it does happen.

Don:

Don told his boss that another department was recruiting him for a big promotion, and he wanted to transfer. Don's boss became furious. "How could you do this to me? How could you betray your own department? I hired you. Don't you have any loyalty, any gratitude?" Don was stunned. He felt terrible for about two days. Then, he decided he didn't want to work for someone who treated him that way. He left within six months.

2. "People Should Know What I Want."

This is an understandable response, but a pretty feeble one. The fact is people probably don't know unless you ask, and ask clearly. And it doesn't really count that you asked if the people you asked didn't hear the question.

MBA Student:

A graduating MBA student called me from the road following his marathon set of interviews for jobs. "The last one's the one I want. I really hope I get it."

"Did you tell them you want it? Did you ask for the job offer?" I replied.

"I didn't need to. I told them I was interested. That should have been enough."

"Hang up the phone now and call them right back and ask for the job."

He called back twenty minutes later, very excited. "They told me they were very glad I called. I had been their top candidate. But they weren't sure I was really interested, so if I hadn't called back, I wouldn't have gotten the job."

3. "They Are in Control."

In any organization, in any company, there isn't really a "they." There are only people like the rest of us—real people. "They" are real people, like us, who don't do things perfectly. Real people don't return phone calls when they said they would. Sometimes we don't either. Real people don't explain business strategy clearly. Sometimes we have a hard time explaining things, too. Real people don't give you that promotion you think you deserve. It's possible we would do the same thing if we had the same facts.

When people say "they" instead of "my manager's boss," or "the marketing department," they make real people sound like some sort of ominous and omnipotent force. Who in the world would want to ask anything of that kind of a power?

Real people are much easier to deal with. They are like us. They have many different motives and reasons. When you find out what the reasons are, you may understand what to do to be successful.

Bank Department:

"They never promote people from within." This was the commonly heard complaint about a particular department of a large bank. A small task force of people who wanted internal advancement took a look at who "they" actually were and why they didn't promote people from within. "They" turned out to be the managers who dealt in person with high net worth customers. Most of these managers said that they would prefer to hire internal employees because of their knowledge of the bank.

But the internal applicants were pulling together resumes at the last minute, sometimes with mistakes. They were coming unprepared for the interviews, and acting as if they were entitled to the job no matter what the qualifications were. In addition, they didn't bother to follow the stated dress code for the new jobs.

Once the task force had asked the managers what the problems were and understood the answers, it was easy to teach internal applicants how to improve their chances of being hired in this department.

All of the people in these stories—the task force, the consultant, and the MBA—asked for what they wanted and got an answer that made a difference in their careers and in their work satisfaction. But all of them were coached on how and when to ask. Think of this book as your coach on how to ask for what you want—for the things that will help you become happy and successful at work.

Part I

Think Before You Ask

Larry:

Larry was a manager in a small start-up. He loved his work and the people he worked with, but he was working too hard and traveling too much. Larry was burning out. He wanted to find another company to work for where he could have a better balance in his life.

"Larry," I said, "you say that you love what you are doing. Have you ever thought of asking your boss for what you want?"

Larry had all kinds of reasons why he couldn't ask. "My boss is out straight now. I just couldn't do it to him. He's just lost another manager at my level.

He'll be angry I'm even asking. He believes everyone should work the hours he works. He'll say no."

"But if you are prepared to look elsewhere anyway, why not give your boss a chance? Even if he says no, what have you got to lose?"

Larry agreed. He analyzed what he really wanted. He wanted ten-hour days and one business trip a month. He wanted to be in a role in which he could coach other product managers. He wanted to have a more strategic impact on his company—to use his industry knowledge to influence the direction of the company.

Larry knew that he was even more necessary to his company because one of his colleagues had left. Knowing what the circumstances were and what he really wanted, Larry carefully crafted a presentation to his boss like the ones he used to sell his clients. The presentation included how his boss could restructure his staff so that the work would get done. He had thought through what was in his manager's interest and in the company's interest. He only asked for what he knew the manager could give him.

His logical approach was persuasive with his manager. In return for Larry's promise to continue to *be the point person with the company's biggest customer, the manager agreed to Larry's reorganization plan and promised to help Larry sell his ideas on strategy to senior management.*

Finally, Larry was careful not to make wholesale complaints like, "Everyone around here is burned out. We all need to get a life around here." He just asked for himself.

Larry followed all of the five rules for thinking before you ask:

Rule 1. Know what to ask for

Rule 2. Know when you have
a special opportunity to ask

Rule 3. Make a presentation

Rule 4. Ask for help

Rule 5. Ask for yourself, not for someone else

Know What to Ask For

People have a tendency to have tapped-on-the-shoulder careers. Their bosses or colleagues tap them on the shoulder and say, "How about this?" and a few years later, "How about this?" These people never make a choice for themselves—they just accept what someone else is offering.

- *If you always wait for something to be suggested before you make a choice, you never go through the discipline of deciding what you want for yourself.*

Of course, people frequently don't know what they want. It's a lot easier to say yes to what is presented to you rather than go through the work of figuring out what you want for yourself.

- *If you are having trouble figuring out what you want, pay attention to your own motivation when you are at work.*

What projects are you working on when you are raring to get to work? What are you doing when you are feeling bored and angry? Asking for more of the former and less of the latter only makes sense.

- *Another way to identify what to ask for is to look at obstacles you keep running into.*

An obstacle might be a degree or a credential you lack. It might be a skill you lack, like running meetings, understanding cost accounting, or making presentations. All of those obstacles represent something to ask for.

What you want will change over time. You have to accommodate those changes as they occur. Here are some easy examples: the recent college graduate who wants to take the job with the highest salary possible to pay back college loans; the person whose husband just had a heart attack and doesn't want to travel; the person whose children have finished college and wants to try out that exciting idea for a new business.

Check in with yourself at least every year to assess what you want at that time, so that what you are asking for meets your current needs.

• *Your wants may conflict.*

For example, "I want to see if I would be interested in sales, but I don't want to leave my terrific team." Or, "I can't decide whether I should become more technical or take my business systems analyst skills and become more business-focused." When you can't decide, you should collect more data.

To stick with the previous examples, test out your interest in sales by going on a sales call with one of the best salespeople in your company. Meet with one of the technical gurus in your company and ask questions about what she does. Then, talk to a businessman you respect and ask questions about what he does. If you can't collect the data on your own, ask for the opportunity to collect the data. If you still can't decide, collect more data.

• *Check the reality of what you are asking for.*

Geography can really matter if what you are asking for is a particular kind of work. A very talented documentary producer moved to Boston and started looking for a job. "I've been looking for over a year, and I can't find anything," he complained. Well, there's just not a big documentary filmmaking industry in Boston; New York or Los Angeles would have been better options. Boston is, by contrast, a great place for biotech jobs, university jobs, or mutual fund jobs.

Economic reality also matters. A lot of what people ask their managers for is pay-related. But they rarely check the economic feasibility of what they are asking for. Ask yourself how you are paid relative to the market for your skills. What are the factors that affect your company's pay practices? A 2 percent raise may be a big one in a company that is struggling. You may be asking for something that the person you are asking can't give you. That makes both of you frustrated.

If you are asking your manager for something, it's important to ask for something that is within your manager's power to grant. It's also important to ask for something that provides value not just for you, but for your employer as well.

Look at this diagram to see if what you're asking for fits within the shaded area. If it doesn't, ask for something else.

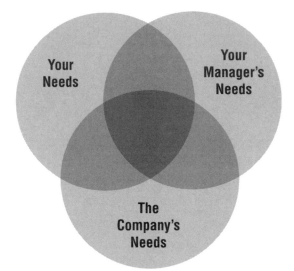

Here's an example. A talented marketing manager found out that her boss's budget didn't allow her to go to a conference on e-commerce, so she asked for an e-commerce course through tuition reimbursement instead. Her boss was able to give her that.

Here are a few typically unrealistic asks and some realistic alternatives to them:

- **Unrealistic Ask 1.**
  "Give me the chance to do this job. I know I could do the job if you would only give it to me."

For most jobs, this is not true. Jobs have real job requirements and before someone hires you to do a job, he or she has to trust that you can do the job. The right credentials and the right experience are a form of proof that you can do the job.

Take the job apart in your mind. Can you prove you have done all the components of the job? If you can, then you have a chance. Otherwise, begin by asking for the job's components.

For example, if you are targeting a job as a first level manager and you have never managed before, ask for the components of managing. In other words, ask if you can be among the interviewers for new hires; ask if you can train or coach them; ask to manage a project or redesign workflow. Once you have had the experience of doing the components of a manager's job, you are a logical candidate when a position becomes available.

- **Unrealistic Ask 2.**
  "Give me the promotion. I deserve it."

This statement may or may not be true when you look at it from another perspective. Are there others who really deserve the same promotion? Would your boss's boss agree? What did the last three people who were promoted do to make themselves eligible for the promotion? With that data, you can decide to pursue asking for a promotion, or delay it until you have made yourself into a candidate with the right credentials.

- **Unrealistic Ask 3.**
  "Give me a raise. I am underpaid."

Are you really? This is easy to check now that people have access to the Internet. Other sources include headhunters, newspaper ads, friends you have in human resources, and surveys done by professional associations in your specialty area. Then, if you really are underpaid, you'll have a lot of data to present that supports your opinion.

Know When You Have
a Special Opportunity to Ask

There are plenty of opportunities for asking for what you want. You just need to be able to identify them. Here are some of the most common situations:

The performance review

Employers create special opportunities to ask as a part of their performance management processes. Don't miss these opportunities. Always ask for professional development of some kind at your performance review. Ask for training or for coaching from a star performer; ask to belong to a professional association, or go to a meeting or a conference; ask to be assigned a special project or to a task force; ask for courses or classes. As a general rule, you should ask for learning opportunities that also increase your personal network or that show others what you can do.

The performance review may also be an ideal time to ask for a promotion or a new assignment to bring out the qualities and talents you really want to use. If you do decide to go this route, make sure you have prepared a really good presentation that takes your manager's self interest into account.

When they want you to stay

The more your managers want to retain you, and the more critical you are to the operation of your department, the more opportunity you have to ask for what you need.

Jeanne:

Jeanne was the only programmer still at a small bank at the time of its merger with a larger one. All of the computer operations of the bank had long since been outsourced, but Jeanne was the only one who knew how the small bank's system related to that of the outsourced vendor's.

When the acquiring bank beseeched her to stay, Jeanne knew she could ask for a lot, and she did. She got a stay-on bonus, a tuition-free master's degree in information technology, and a new job with the acquiring bank.

When they want you to leave

You have a surprising amount of leverage when your organization wants you to leave. Particularly if it was a mistake in hiring. It's always worthwhile to see what arrangement you can negotiate in return for leaving.

Joan:

Joan was an administrative assistant in the wrong job, and she was failing at it. She was on perform-ance warning and suspected that her boss would fire her at the end of the next month when her per-formance warning ran out.

Joan offered her boss a deal. In return for a rea-sonable reference, salary continuance for two months, and some outplacement help, she would turn over her work to others and leave right away. Her boss only gave her the reference and one month of salary continuance, but Joan had enough of a cushion to look for another job.

When you are being apologized to

If you are about to be apologized to, make sure you have something you can ask for. You are more than likely to get it.

Dean:

Dean was recruited to work for a "great" man who had a reputation for throwing temper tantrums and verbally abusing his staff. When the human resources director interviewed him, Dean mentioned his future manager's reputation. "Oh, that won't happen anymore," she assured Dean. "We've sent him to all kinds of special training."

Three months and many temper tantrums later, Dean was back in the HR director's office. "I'm so sorry," she said.

Dean was prepared. He knew that the apology was his cue to ask. Dean asked for six months' salary continuance, great references, and outplacement help. The firm was so concerned about its reputation that Dean got what he wanted.

When you have gotten recognition for having worked very hard on something

The key in this case is the word recognition. Without

the recognition, your chance to ask successfully will decrease. After all, if a tree falls in the woods and no one is around to notice...

When you get that departmental award, when you get a big public thank you from one of your important customers, when you are recognized at the launch party for that job you did on project implementation—all are times when you should think about what opportunity it would be appropriate to ask for.

Make a Presentation

If you have something important to ask for, take the time to prepare. You'll be more likely to get a yes answer. When you've been thinking about something for a long time, like that raise or promotion, it probably doesn't feel impulsive to you when you blurt it out in your boss's office one morning. But it might feel like a surprise to her. She might feel as if she is being put on the spot. And when people feel put on the spot, their first impulse is to say no.

Whether you are interviewing for a job or participating in a performance appraisal, think through what you are going to say, and in particular, what you are going to ask for. The more prepared you are, the more spontaneous you will seem. That great motivational speaker, basketball player, and singer all have practice and hard work in common. Fully prepared, they can respond to whatever happens in the moment.

Practice your presentation with a friend. Ask your friend to think up questions or concerns that the person you are presenting to may have. Then, practice the answers to those questions. Remember to identify the self-interest of the person you are talking to. Don't just talk about yourself and what you need—talk about how that need benefits the company.

Generally speaking, the more formal the presentation you make, the more serious and committed you look. In some industries and jobs, such as biotech or academia, formal presentations are a normal part of the hiring process. Ten beautifully crafted PowerPoint slides might be overkill in some circles, but a page with four or five bullet points might not be. Just as you should dress up a little more formally for a job interview than you would on the job, you should aim for a presentation style that is a little more formal than your usual style.

Nora:

When Nora had her second child, she realized that

continuing in her fast-paced sales job was a recipe for burnout. Using the format her company used for sales presentations to customers, Nora put together a formal presentation in which she asked for a new, less demanding position. She included an estimate of the revenue she would be able to bring in with the new job, her new job description, what she would do to hire a replacement salesperson for her old job, and the dollar value of the redesigned positions to her company. She got what she wanted.

Ask for Help

A sking for help is hard for many people. They would much prefer to be the helper than the helpee. Asking for help somehow makes them feel less important, less professional, less in charge.

Ironically, the opposite is generally true. When you ask for help in association with what you are asking for, it doesn't seem like so much of a demand to either you or the person you are asking. It seems like more of a collaborative effort. Just listen to how this sounds to you:

"I'd like a promotion." vs. "I'd like your help in becoming a great candidate for the next promotion."

"I want more senior management visibility." vs.

"Would you be willing to coach me on how to become more recognized and respected by senior management?"

Asking for help is a great way to get to know customers, colleagues, and subordinates. People are flattered when you ask them because that means you chose to ask them instead of someone else.

It's a great way to defuse tense situations, too.

Leon:

Leon was new to his company. He was hired into a department to "bring it into the twenty-first century." But his whole department was disgruntled and muttering, "They never promote people from within. What about Karen? She would have done a fine job if only they had given her a chance."

Leon went to see Karen and said, "I'm new here and need your help." He told her that he would teach her his technical skills in exchange for her help in modernizing the department. She agreed. He taught her what he knew, which increased her marketability. She helped him learn the functions of the department so that he was successful in modernizing it.

*Ask for Yourself,
Not for Someone Else*

There are times when you are supposed to represent the opinions of others. Many labor relations or audit jobs require that you serve as an advocate for others. Also, people on multidisciplinary task forces frequently are supposed to represent the opinions of others.

But in general, when you are asking for something for yourself, adding more people to the situation only makes things more difficult.

Here are a few reasons why.

It can sound like complaining.
For example, "Our whole department is just not up to

date in terms of project management skills and software. We'll never have the credibility we need with the line organization until we do." vs. "I want to be an excellent project manager. I'd like a chance to learn the Super Duper System and see if it would make a difference here."

The others you are speaking for should be present, or they may back out or change their minds.

For example, "Allen and I really feel we need some more product training." Only to have Allen say later, "You may need some training, but I really understand our products."

It is more difficult for a person to say yes to a group demand.

For example, "We all agree that we have been working really long hours here. We need comp time so that we can take some time off when we work so much overtime." vs. "I'm really burned out. Can I take a half day off next Tuesday to catch up on my sleep and my laundry?" The second question is limited, and so the request can be accommodated.

More importantly, you are treating the person you are asking as a real person with discretion, not as an authority figure—as one of the "theys". When you treat people as real people, they will respond as real people. When you treat people as authority figures, they will respond as authority figures.

Sometimes it is true that everyone in the office feels the same way as you do. In those cases, each person should ask the manager—individually—for the same thing. Then, the manager might understand that everyone needs a little time off.

When you ask for what you want, you are acknowledging to yourself and to others that you are a person who must be taken seriously.

Part II

The Answers and What They Mean

One of the reasons people don't ask is because they don't know what to do with the possible answers they might get. Before you actually ask for what you want, you should take a minute to play out possible responses. While it may seem like over-preparation, it will make you much more confident. Even salespeople who are used to asking for the sale and who are prepared carefully for all the responses they may get, rarely take the time to prepare when the product they are selling is themselves.

Here are the possible answers and some ideas about what they mean, so you will have a framework for how to respond when you hear the answer.

The Answer: No

Here are two no stories:

Steven:

Steven worked very hard to collect the data that would prove his boss's contention that the financial services firm they worked for was missing out on a really lucrative market opportunity for a new financial product. The data made Steven a convert to the idea, so he was there and committed when his boss, Andrew, presented his findings to the senior marketing committee.

The committee disagreed with the research and

refused to put any more resources into the new direction—a real, loud no.

Both men were not only disappointed and frustrated but now became concerned that they had a new reputation for presenting ideas that would fail. Andrew couldn't stand it and left the company within the year.

Steven, however, really believed his research. Other firms were working on the product. He knew that as a leading firm in the industry, his firm would sooner or later have to follow what its competitors were doing. Customers would ask for the new product. Sooner or later his firm would have to offer it.

So, Steven treated the no as a maybe later. He continued to collect data on the market he had researched. He took note of when his firm's competitors started to move into the market. He networked his way around his own organization showing the data he had collected and asking people if they thought their organization should offer this new product. He also asked for data that showed that their own customers were clamoring for the new product.

After three years, interest was building around the organization for the product. With a base of support for the idea, Steven got a chance for a second presentation. This time the committee said yes and gave Steven a big promotion.

Anne:

Anne was the highest ranking woman manager in her bank. When her bank was sold to a bigger one, she made some money on her stock, but was out of a job.

Her new boss in the acquiring bank sat her down for a talk about her future. "People like you are one of the reasons we bought this bank. We believe you are a very talented person that we want to keep and develop in our new combined organization. Because of our growth, we have lots of opportunity. Take some time. Look over our openings. Meet people in our bank. Talk to a career coach. Come back and propose to us what you would really like to do next."

Anne did exactly that. She came back and made a presentation that went: "My strengths are in making operations more productive and in influencing people to try something new. I involve others in rethinking operational processes and in choosing the right technology. Then, I follow through with people so that the implementation of any new system goes well. I've talked to both the business analysts in your systems department and the operations analysts in your productivity department. I think I belong on the business side, but either department would be a great assignment. The people I have talked with think that to become a director or a vice president, I would need to sharpen my financial skills, so that is what I would like to learn next. So what I'd like to ask for is a business analyst position and training in financial management."

The answer came back. "That was a great presentation. You did your homework, but those positions are all filled now. Make another proposal."

So Anne did. And got the same response. By this time, she had met a lot of people in the acquiring bank. Surely if there had been a good position for her, someone would have told her. So, she decided their yes was really a no and found a new position elsewhere.

The moral of these stories is that sometimes no really means maybe later and sometimes what sounds like yes really means no. So, you can't always tell if the answer you have gotten will be the complete and total answer.

The most important thing to do when you hear a negative answer is to train yourself to pay attention to the other point of view. This does not mean imagining their reasons! For example, don't conclude "He never liked me," or, "It's all political." It means asking them enough questions so that you understand their point of view.

With that data, you can figure out why you got the no response and what the response really means. Then, you can use your own judgement to assess whether it makes sense to ask again later, like Steven, or to move on the way Andrew did. Most people faced with a no would move on. It is far easier to accept the negative answer, even when you are disappointed, than it is to try again. But if you can put your feelings aside, as Stephen did, you can analyze your chances on that second try.

The no that Anne got is much harder to deal with. Yes means yes at least 85 percent of the time. But until you actually follow up on the response, you don't know whether your yes is in the really no 15 percent or not.

In many organizations, it's common for people to be reluctant to give bad news. So, if the positive answer is followed by negative actions, or no action at all, it's important to pay attention to what people do, not what people say.

In Anne's case, she ended up believing that there were some people who really did want her to join the big bank. But there were others who were just going through the motions and were unwilling to express their disagreement. Once she believed that was the true reason, she knew she should leave.

The Answer: No Response

Most people assume that if they don't get an answer to a request, the answer is no. They sometimes even make up answers in place of getting no response. A transfer candidate might be thinking, "The reason I haven't heard about my transfer is that I'm just not the right person for the assignment," when in fact, the person handling the transfer is on vacation.

While it is true that most people avoid telling bad news like, "You're not going to get that promotion," it is still worth being persistent. Even if you think the chances are low that you will get a positive response, keep trying until you get either an answer or so many no responses that you don't want to continue asking.

Because so many no response answers occur to people during the hiring process, both of the examples that follow are hiring examples of getting no response. Just remember that you can also get no response to a request to go to a special conference, to take a course, or when you ask for a promotion. The principle of how long to follow up is the same.

Jake:

Jake was a talented mechanical engineer in a senior management position in a manufacturing plant. He knew the plant would close in nine months, so Jake scrambled to find another position. Early on, a friend gave him a lead to a position in the manufacturing arm of a high tech firm. The interviews went well. He felt as if he was only days away from an offer. But nothing happened. He called and called. He got angry and frustrated and extended his search beyond this firm. But, he kept persisting. Every week or so, he would send an email to one of the people who had interviewed him expressing his contin-

ued interest in the job. He didn't make the mistake of counting on this job to come through, but he didn't drop it either.

About three months later, he got a call. Was he still on the job market? The firm had gone through a major restructuring which had stopped the hiring process, but now that it was over, they were considering him for a new position. After all, they knew from his emails he was very interested in the company. This time, Jake got the job offer in two weeks.

Angela:

By contrast, Angela, although she was persistent, put all her eggs in one basket—the one employer she wanted to work for.

After years of being based on the East Coast, Angela moved back to the West Coast because of a serious family illness. She was sure that she would do well in the job market because of her skills and experience.

Although she didn't have much of a network on the West Coast, she managed to get an interview with her target company. Her initial interview went very well. "Oh, we are bound to have lots of jobs

that you would be perfect for," said the first inter-
viewer. She sent Angela's resume to four or five hir-
ing managers.

One by one, Angela followed up, and one by
one, she got no response. In each case, the first
interview would go fine. Then there would be other
interviews to schedule and people to meet. Delays
would occur. She would follow up. Interviews
would be canceled. She would hear something
mildly positive and then, nothing.

As the process stretched out, Angela began to
doubt herself. Was she too old? Too East Coast in
style? Too experienced? Not experienced enough?
Should she revise her resume? Change her inter-
view approach? Her self-doubt showed in the inter-
view process, making it even more unlikely that she
would be successful in her job search. Ultimately,
Angela's friends turned her around. She did what
she should have done earlier. She changed her tar-
get employer, broadened her job search, and found
a good job.

It's impossible to tell in advance whether no
response will turn out to be a no or a yes. You are not
in control. What you are in control of is how you

respond personally. Not getting an answer can be very frustrating. Yes, it is impolite and uncaring not to answer a reasonable request. But, that being said, it's up to you to follow up anyway. When you get to the point where the lack of response is causing you to doubt yourself, that's the time you should move on.

In Angela's case, anything could have caused the delays—bureaucracy in the hiring process, internal applicants, or any number of other things could have happened that Angela didn't know about. What was really happening wasn't nearly as important as what was happening to Angela. Moving on gave her back her feeling of being in control.

The Answer: Yes, But...

Most people's immediate response when they hear a "yes, but" answer is to forget the but. It's hard when you hear a yes not to get so excited that you forget to remember exactly what the but is.

The "but" represents conditions you must pay attention to if you are to get what you requested. If you aren't sure what the conditions are, it's perfectly all right to ask for clarification.

Generally speaking, the more you can involve your management and colleagues in fulfilling these conditions, the more successful you will be at meeting them. Dana is an example.

Dana:

Dana had been looking for the opportunity to manage a large and complex project. After he asked his manager, he got a big assignment with a big "but".

The story went something like this: "Dana, we know how talented and ambitious you are. We are offering you a plum project with a lot of visibility. It is to design and implement a global financial information system. If you do it well, your career future is assured. It is, however, a really tough assignment, and you know how stretched resources are right now. You'll just have to figure out how to do the project and do your current job as well."

Dana had always been motivated by challenge. He knew he had a lot of energy. So he tried to do both jobs. His first idea was to work more hours. That wasn't effective. The more hours he worked, the more tired he became and the more he was afraid he would make an error. So, he started double and triple checking his work, which took more time, and the vicious cycle started over again. Dana was burning out. Dana had heard the yes, but he hadn't heard the but. He hadn't stopped to figure out how to do the new assignment and his current job at the same time.

Fortunately, his boss, Bob, caught on early. "Your approach is just not going to work," he said. "Let me work with you to come up with a plan for doing what needs to be done, delegating the rest, and involving others. You need to ask for help. You need to set priorities. Think it through first!"

Together, Bob and Dana identified parts of his current job that were low priority and delegated some things and deferred others until the new project was over. Then, with Bob's help, Dana put together a task force of people who had a stake in the outcome of the global financial system. The task force and Dana put together a project plan with deadlines and deliverables that everyone needed to meet. Because the members of the task force all had a stake in the success of the project, they all helped get the work done. That was how Dana really learned project management.

Living with Yes as an Answer

When you ask for something and you get it, without conditions, it can be something of a shock. Particularly if you have been asking for it for a while. Sometimes, the yes is so long in coming that it feels like an anticlimax. But it probably hasn't lost its meaning to the person who is offering it. If you act bored or as if you have deserved it for a long time, you're running the danger of not getting what you ask for the next time.

If you hear a yes, just like candidates on election night, you need to be ready with an acceptance speech. Part of that acceptance speech should be a thank you, an acknowledgement of the effort involved in getting you what you asked for, and your commitment to the future. Here's an example of such an acceptance speech:

"Thank you, Marty. That's great. I am very happy about my title change to Director of Product Marketing from Product Marketing Manager. This isn't a company that likes to give people titles, so I know you had to be persuasive to get it for me. You can be sure that when I'm at customer sites, I'll make the most of this new title to build relationships with senior management."

When you are given what you ask for, you are then obliged to go forward with your new commitment, unless you have a really good excuse. That's why it's so important to know what you want when you ask.

If you get what you ask for, there is an obligation that goes with that answer. Companies that sponsor employees for an MBA usually require them to stay with the company for a couple of years after they complete their degrees. A request for more responsibility will mean that you will have more to pay attention to. If you are granted that additional staff member you asked for, you'll have to get started on the hiring process, and so forth.

One yes from a manager is likely to get you a second yes if you follow through on your part of the deal. Developing a pattern of asking and getting yes's with your boss will result in greater career development opportunities on the job. Jane's story is one such example.

Jane:

Jane is an attorney who worked in the corporate legal department of a large manufacturing firm. Her primary work was reviewing contracts after they had been negotiated. She knew she could contribute to the negotiations, but she felt she was pigeonholed as a contracts person. She wasn't able to offer credible business advice before the deals were made.

She made a good case and documented it carefully, so her manager agreed to sponsor her for an executive MBA. Once the manager made the commitment, he was easily persuaded to give Jane work assignments that capitalized on what she was learning in her MBA program. Within a year, she had asked for and gotten a spot on the negotiating team.

The Wrong Answer:
When the Manager Isn't Listening
and Gives You Money
Instead of What You Really Want

Managers expect to be asked for promotions and for money, so if they are asked for something else, they may not hear it. They assume they know what an employee wants and that it's always money, or that no matter what the problem is, it can be resolved with money. That kind of answer may not solve your primary concern.

Claire:

Claire had a nasty commute and a great job. Because of her special knowledge and because she was such a team player, she had been very successful. In a career field in which an MBA was com-

mon, she didn't even have a BA. She was paid about $10,000 a year less than people in comparable jobs in the company were.

In terms of her personal goals, she had recently married and was looking forward to having children. But her workday was long, not just because of her commute, but also because her manager insisted she be there whenever he needed her. Often, that meant ten to twelve hour days. Claire made the decision to resign, get a job closer to home, go to school part time, and think about getting pregnant.

When she talked to her boss, Al, he panicked and called in the human resources generalist that supported his area. "Give her a $20,000 bonus," he said.

"Let me talk to her," said the HR person.

Claire and the human resources generalist crafted a set of conditions that would allow Claire to stay and meet all of her personal goals: tuition reimbursement to a special MBA program, an assistant she could train to take over a portion of her job, a raise of $10,000, and a guarantee that she could leave every evening at 5 P.M. and at 3 P.M. on Wednesdays so that she would be able to attend the MBA program.

"Al might agree to the tuition reimbursement and the assistant but he will never agree to letting me leave at five," she said to the HR person. *"He likes to have me available whenever he is free."*

Al did agree, via email. But Claire wanted him to agree in person.

"OK," he replied. *"Meet me in my office at 4 P.M. today."* Claire went to his office, but his door was closed. She waited and waited. At 6:30, the door was still closed. When he came out at 7:15, Claire had left. She knew he wasn't prepared to let her leave at 5:00 for her MBA program.*

It is always worthwhile to negotiate for what you want, even if it doesn't work out. Claire did a great job of being clear about what she wanted and really persisted. For this kind of manager, who himself was probably motivated only by money, it was realistic to anticipate that he wouldn't change. If she had chosen to stay and take the salary and MBA sponsorship, she could expect that every time she was ready to leave at 5:00, her boss would come up with something critical for her to do. If she wasn't prepared to fight that fight on a regular basis, it was reasonable to look somewhere else.

When to Just Do It Without Asking

The key to being trusted is being predictably reliable. Then you are likely to be offered a lot of independence and with that independence, a chance to exercise your own judgement and grow in your assignments.

There will be times in your career when it is important to act without asking. In fact, if you don't ever take action without asking, you're probably being too conservative. But if you are a person who is trusted, that won't matter. It won't be a bet-your-career type of situation.

Learning when you can act without asking is a necessary skill. Every time you make a transition from one boss to another, you have to renegotiate how much autonomy you have. The basic objective you should have in your mind is to get the greatest freedom of action you can, so that you are only asking your boss for important things. With greater freedom of action, you have more time and more opportunity to learn and to grow. When you are not micromanaged, both you and your manager have more time to get real work done.

If you remember that the degree to which you are micromanaged is directly related to the amount of fear your manager feels, then you will know how to build your credibility to act on your own. You should get approval in advance and operate on that approval. Here are some examples:

"Here is my project plan for the project. It includes major milestones and the times I will be checking in with you. Is that OK?"

"Here is a list of people I will be contacting for the survey. If you would like to change or add any names, please let me know by Friday."

"I am currently planning to go ahead with the acquisition we discussed at the meeting last week. If we are successful or if something changes I will be sure to let you know."

Here are some common situations in which you can anticipate that just doing it without checking with your boss can lead to trouble, and some ideas for how to re-establish your reputation.

When you are new to a position or to a manager

You always have to earn your independence. Try asking how the manager likes to be updated on what you are doing. Check in more often than you think is reasonable and ask for feedback. "Is this the kind of decision you want me to refer to you?" "Who needs to agree before we can go ahead?" "The next time I have the same kind of customer problem, should I just solve it in the same way?"

Even if you are a new CEO, this approach is a good one, although you should always present yourself as asking for an endorsement, not delegating a decision. "This would be my approach. What do you think? Would you agree?"

When you have just screwed up

Whether one mistake will cost you your credibility or not depends upon the style of your bosses you work for and the size of the mistake. The bigger the problem, the more likely it is to impact their trust in you. If you have been trusted to operate on your own in the past, the recovery time will be fast. But expect to be managed tightly until you are trusted again.

In a crisis

Most managers will move in and take over when there is a crisis. This is more likely to be true when they have caused the crisis themselves. In this situation, as in the others above, the manager is afraid of failure. It will not make your manager more confident in you if you ask your manager to back off. Your manager will only feel more out of control.

The right approach is to build your manager's confidence in your reliability. For example, you might say, "I'll take care of this the way I did the last time the line went down." If you really need some space, give your manager something to do like, "I'll check these graphs while you proofread those slides." Working along side of you, your manager will feel more secure.

Part III

Ask ALL the Right People

Now you have thought through what you are going to ask for and have prepared yourself for the possible answers you could get. As the number of manager-related examples in Part II suggests, your manager can be very important in helping you manage your career.

When your manager is naturally a mentor or a coach, you will find it easy to ask your manager for what you need. But in this era of rapid change, no matter how carefully you selected the person you are working for, your manager is likely to change at least every year or two. It's harder to ask for what you need from someone you don't know well. If your manager doesn't know you or isn't receptive, you still have other options. Your manager is not the only person you should ask. It is also important to consider all the other people you could ask who might be helpful to your career.

Ask Your Customers

The customer service movement has made the internal and external customers for your work more important to your career. Most people, like salespeople, customer service reps, and marketing folks, are aware of how important satisfied customers are to the success of a business and to their own success as individuals. If you are in an accounting, human resources, tech support, or information technology department, you have customers, too. It's just that they are internal to the company you both work for.

When firms are assessing an individual's performance, many now regularly ask for feedback from both kinds of customers—internal and external. If your customers think you are wonderful, that can influence how the people above you view you. All it takes is a little initiative from you to get positive results. Just ask, as Janet did.

Janet:

Janet was new to her job as divisional controller and was concerned about how her superiors viewed her. When one of the vice presidents in her division complimented her profusely on her help during the budget cycle, she asked him if he would mind putting that compliment in an email to her boss. He didn't mind, and Janet's reputation was assured.

Customers are also great sources for information. And using information wisely is one good strategy for managing your career. Here are a few examples:

George:

George was a young financial analyst responsible for producing monthly reports. He took the initiative to ask the people he sent the reports to for their input. What reports were helpful? Were there any that weren't helpful? Were there any additional features that might be helpful?

George used the data to prepare a presentation to his boss about how George might make those reports user-friendly. His boss agreed with many of his points and George developed a great reputation not only with his customers, but also with his boss.

Tara:

Tara was a star teller at her bank. She never lost her cool with customers. She was unfailingly polite, courteous, and accurate. Customers would stand in her line, even if other tellers were free.

One day, a regular customer of hers asked, "What are you going to do next in your career? Are you going to stay in banking?" Tara answered that she had always dreamed of a career in high tech but, in spite of her night courses in computers, she had not been able to find the right job. Then she asked, "Do you have any suggestions for me?"

Her customer replied, "With your accuracy and customer service skills, you ought to be able to get a job in tech support. I have a friend who is looking for people for tech support and is willing to train them. I'd be happy to give him a call for you."

Tom:

Tom was the lead salesman for a company that made equipment for specialty manufacturers. His job involved helping to make sure the equipment was used correctly, and he was so good at the job that his customers loved him. As the industry that Tom served declined, he realized that he'd better start selling more than one product line if he expected to have a long career. But, like many of us, Tom was satisfied enough with his current job to put off looking again and again.

Two years ago, when his company sold his product line to another firm, Tom saw the opportunity to get what he wanted. He went to the acquiring company and asked for a deal—he would retain his client base for them in return for the assignment to sell other products to the same customers. The new company had other, more up-to-date products for Tom to sell and agreed. "If you retain 90 percent of your customers by the end of six months," his new boss assured him, "we'll give you other products to sell, plus a big bonus."

After six months, Tom had completed his part of the bargain, but the new company had reneged on theirs. His boss stormed into Tom's office, fired him

*on the spot, and took possession of his computer
with all his customer contact information on it. Tom
was devastated—and angry.*

*Although Tom didn't have a job, he had some
valuable assets. He had strong relationships with his
customers, and he had made good friends wherever
he had worked. First, Tom recontacted his largest
customers and asked for their support and help.
Then, he called his friends at his old company and
asked for the same thing.*

*When they found out he had been fired, friends
at his old company gave Tom a copy of his customer
database from the year before. Armed with his database and the confidence of his customers, Tom went
to a major competitor of the company that had fired
him and asked for a job. They picked him up imme-
diately, this time with the option of selling a whole
line of products.*

What all these customer stories have in common is
that they are not what most people would call net-
working stories. In each case, the person in the story
had a genuine reputation for service excellence.
These are not do-me-a-favor stories; they are stories of
people who had done such a good job of customer

satisfaction that their customers were willing to do
something in return for them.

Vendors Are Customers, Too

In the past, vendors were handled almost entirely by purchasing agents and were never trusted. Now partnership relationships between vendor and customer are increasingly frequent. They require much more mutual cooperation and trust.

Now all kinds of services are outsourced to vendors. Outsourcing and purchasing decisions are also made lower down in organizations than they used to be. Managers in all parts of a business may be doing the calculations that determine whether outsourcing is a good option, reviewing and choosing vendors, and monitoring vendor contracts.

Vendors have a particular interest in helping to

advance the careers of the people who have chosen to use them. If a printer helps a talented graphic designer get a position at a different advertising firm, the designer is highly likely to use the printer again in the new firm.

Vendors work across a group of employers who purchase their services and products. They know a lot about the corporate culture at different places. They are frequently among the first people asked for referrals when there is a new opening. Also, if you are referred to a new job by one of the vendors who work with you, it is easy for the new company to assume that you are good at what you do. Vendors will never refer a turkey—that would surely reflect poorly on them.

Vendors generally know what is hot in your field and who is doing something interesting. They are usually very willing to share, but only if you treat them as well as you would treat customers. Yes, it is true, you are their customer, but a true customer relationship works both ways. Respect increases respect.

Kevin:

Kevin was a human resources director in charge of recruitment. The rule in his company was that if a headhunter had presented a candidate's resume to you and you had rejected it, and after more than six months you hired that same candidate for a different job, you didn't need to pay the headhunter's fee.

All of the headhunters who worked with Kevin knew the rules. But one time, Kevin actually paid a fee he didn't have to. Of course, Kevin had to explain it to his boss. He explained it was only the fair thing to do. "The headhunter reminded me that we had really liked the candidate and it was only a day or two over the six month rule, so we should pay the fee."

Kevin's boss agreed. The headhunter was so grateful that he introduced Kevin to another human resources professional who showed Kevin an efficient new applicant tracking system. When Kevin brought that system back to his own company, he was considered a hero.

Disrespect also increases disrespect.

Pat:
Pat was a marketing vice president with a big budget and a short fuse. She screamed at the

vendors who worked for her—all of them, whether they were designers, printers, or ad agencies. She changed her mind and made them do things over and over. She nagged them about their invoices and held up their payments. Her company was so big and so important that most of her vendors groaned but continued to deal with her.

Then, Pat was caught in a major layoff. Her big budget and her powerful position were gone. But her reputation stayed with her. When she asked her vendors for referrals to new jobs and companies, they just said they didn't know of anything. Eventually, she had to move to another city to get a good job. Her vendors didn't help her find a new job, and if they were asked for references, they told the truth. They never wanted to work for her again.

Ask Your Colleagues and Team Members

Colleagues are more important to a person's career than they used to be. Since more work is done in teams, and especially in crossfunctional or project teams, your reputation as a team member can influence the course of your career, both positively and negatively.

There are all kinds of ways that asking your colleagues can help you. You can ask for coaching on something that is hard for you to do. You can ask for feedback on something you have done. You can ask for information about jobs, departments, courses, and bosses. Your colleagues can put you in the best position for a promotion or a job change. Sometimes, when a boss is unable or unwilling to give you what you want, you can still get what you want through your friends. Here is an example:

Paul:

Paul had been a liberal arts major so, five years into his business career, he became concerned about his lack of financial knowledge. He asked his manager to send him to a financial management class. "But you're not a manager, Paul," was the response. "You don't manage any money."

Paul was on a crossfunctional team with Noreen, a member of the controller's staff, and he asked her for help. She was more than willing. In time, he learned Excel and volunteered to manage the team's project budget under Noreen's direction. He then showed his spread sheets to his own department and got people in his own department to give him ideas on how to make them more useful. His manager was pleased and impressed. But even if she hadn't been, Paul had the knowledge he sought and a reputation for being good with numbers—in spite of his liberal arts degree.

Ask the People Who Work for You

Don't forget the people who work for you. They are also people who can make a difference to your career. Many people get hung up about who is reporting to whom and miss a great source of knowledge and professional development—even an opportunity for sales. Here is one such example:

Case Study:
A successful public relations firm had a difficult time attracting and retaining people. They were losing people because their clients were hiring away the firm's young professionals. The CEO of the firm

only saw this as a problem and worked hard to pre-vent the clients from luring away the firm's talent.

Other consulting firms, by contrast, encourage their young professionals to move to jobs in their client companies. Former employees, if they have been treated well, make great customers.

Why not ask former subordinates for business? They know you and your strengths better than anyone docs. All the people who work with you, whether they have been in the past subordinates or bosses or colleagues or customers, all have a part in making you successful and happy at work.

Part IV

If You Are the One Being Asked...

Being asked for something is a compliment. If someone asks you for your help, it is because you are the kind of person that people trust. Here are some guidelines to help you before you respond:

- You can always defer your answer.

- Even when there is a conflict, don't lie.

- Is there an answer that meets your needs, too?

- You don't have to have all the answers.

- Be clear and direct about what you can and cannot do.

- There is always something you can say yes to.

- Pay attention to how you are feeling.

You Can Always Defer Your Answer

You don't have to answer on the spot. Sometimes you need to do some research before you can decide on the appropriate response. You may have to get the approval of your own boss, for example. Or, you might want to think about alternative answers.

Follow these rules for putting off the answer:

- Set a date and time, and don't change it.

- Prepare in advance any questions you are going to ask or any information you need.

- When you do meet, don't just talk—listen. You should not be talking for more than 50 percent of the time.

The best possible preparation is to know what people want before they ask you. That's a core principle of excellent customer service. And, as any salesperson will tell you, the best way to find out what your customers need is to ask them yourself.

Paying careful attention and letting the other person talk are signs of respect and self-assurance. If you are not prepared, or if they have been scheduled and rescheduled, it will feel like a put down to the person asking. It is how you treat the person more than the answer you give that determines how you will be regarded.

Even When There Is a Conflict, Don't Lie

This is a good general principle for everyone. But there are times at work when it can be tempting to say I don't know, when you do know, or to respond with a little white lie. Your credibility is an important asset, more important than taking the easy way out.

In some professions—internal security, audit, human resources, new business development—confidentiality is a professional requirement. Telling a lie, shading the truth, or revealing something confidential can injure your career. If you are in these professions, it is easy to say that you know, but that the information is confidential.

Where the conflict between telling a lie and telling the hard truth becomes really difficult at work is when you are a manager. That is because, as a manager, you represent the organization you work for. You are expected to follow the party line. But it's important to remember that you are not some kind of robot repeating the words of your superiors. Nor are you a corporate Che Guevara representing the point of view of the oppressed. What you are paid to do is to think and to exercise your own best judgement.

The classic example of telling what you know, versus saying what managers are supposed to say, appeared in the *New York Times* during the recession of the '90s in a series of articles called "The Downsizing of America." In the fifth article of the series, a manager was asked by someone working for him if his job was secure. The employee was thinking of buying a house and wondered if he should be getting into real estate at that time.

The manager knew his employee would be laid off but, following corporate instructions, gave no indication that the company had already decided to close the office and the person's job was as good as gone. Then later, after the downsizing, the manager felt guilty about lying to the employee.

At that time, I surveyed about fifty managers about how they would handle a situation like this one. Forty-eight of the fifty didn't just follow the party line the way the manager in the *New York Times* story did. They did something to point the person who asked in the direction of the truth. For example, one of the managers I surveyed suggested replying to the question with a question.

"The fact that you are asking me this means you have some concerns about our company's financial future. What are the indicators you see that might mean a layoff is coming? In the light of what you are telling me, do you think this is a good time to make a major investment?"

Companies come and go. Jobs come and go. But lies last forever in the minds of people who have been lied to.

Is There an Answer That Meets Your Needs, Too?

You don't have to flatly accept or reject any request. You can treat any request as the beginning point in a negotiation in which you, as well as the person who is doing the asking, have something to gain. It is altruistic to help others who need your help. But as Edmund O. Wilson and others have pointed out, whole societies are founded on reciprocal altruism.

Here are a few examples of how that works:

Examples:
Your colleague asks for your help in constructing a budget for a new project of his. You agree to help,

and also to show him how to budget for projects like that one, in return for an introduction to his boss and a little of the credit.

Your boss wants you to take on additional responsibilities in a new field. You agree, in return for permission to go to a conference that will prepare you for the new field.

Someone who works for you wants training in a new software package. You say yes, in return for her coaching the rest of your staff in how to use the program.

One of your staff wants to transfer to a new job outside of your department even though he hasn't worked for you for the six months required by personnel policies. You agree, in return for delaying his start in the new area for a month, and for helping you hire and train his replacement.

You Don't Have to Have
ALL the Answers

Many people look to managers to have all the answers. So, as a result, managers think that they are supposed to have all the answers. That's just not realistic. So, if you are a manager, and there is a concern you have or information you need in order to reply to a request, you can always ask for help in constructing a solution that meets everyone's needs. The easy way to do that is to involve the person asking you for that help. Here is an example:

Paula:

Paula was going crazy with her commute, although she loved the job and the people. So she asked

Max, her boss, if she could work one day a week at home. Max knew, but Paula didn't, that Louisa, the vice president, thought that working from home was a sham, and that people who did it were deadbeats looking to scrounge a few extra hours of free time from the company.

Max also knew it was just a matter of time before Paula would burn out because of her commute and look for a new job. And Paula made real contributions to the department. Max didn't have the perfect answer that would both accommodate Paula and satisfy Louisa, so he chose to involve Paula.

Together, he and Paula made a list of the questions that Louisa was likely to ask and brainstormed ways to overcome her objections.

They made the presentation to Louisa together. Louisa also made a contribution to the ultimate solution. She agreed to a three-month trial with an option to renew, if all went well. Instead of coming up with his own answer, Max had involved both people who had an interest in the solution and came up with an answer that they both agreed to.

Be Clear and Direct About What You Can and Cannot Do

It is very tempting to make promises in the short term that you might not be able to keep, particularly if you are being pushed to do so. Limit your promises to what you are certain you can deliver on. Your credibility depends upon your reputation for doing what you say you will do. Here is an example of a boss who promised something beyond his power and then lost credibility:

Katherine:
Katherine wanted a promotion. Her boss, Bob, held it out for her as an attainable objective, saying that it was hers if she landed that big customer account.

When she came close to accomplishing that "if only," Bob presented her with another one. "When you have converted that big customer on to the system and trained all of them on our system." When she had accomplished that task, he came up with another one. "When you have set up the call center to take care of that account's customer inquiries."

To Katherine, it began to feel like she was six-years-old again and the swimming instructor was saying, "Just swim to me, Katherine," but when she got there, he'd back up a few steps.

What she didn't know was that Bob knew he couldn't promote her, but couldn't bring himself to tell her and risk losing her from the department. Ultimately, Katherine figured it out, went around Bob, and moved to another department. From her new position, Katherine recruited the best talent in Bob's department to work for her saying, "Don't believe anything he says." If he had been honest and helped her make the move up, Bob might have lost Katherine but he would have retained his other key players and his reputation.

If you are concerned about whether the person who asked you for something will misinterpret what you have said, it might make sense to send a confirming email to repeat what you have agreed to. Here is an example of a confirming email to a person who wants a promotion:

"Thank you for the very productive meeting we had yesterday. I am very happy that you are interested in becoming a senior analyst in this department. You make a real contribution to the team. As we agreed, you will be considered for this position again in six months, after you have worked on the Complexity Project and taken the course we discussed. As you know, the new position will not only depend upon what you do to improve your skills, but also upon the continued success of our firm. Let me know what I can do in the next six months to help you achieve your goals."

There Is Always Something You Can Say Yes To

If you are completely stuck, if you have nothing you can give, if you have no resources, there is still something you can say yes to. All it takes is a little creative thinking. Here's an example:

Carol Ann:

Carol Ann was very upset. Donna, the vice president of human resources, had promised Carol Ann a human resources generalist position. But now, her company was going through a layoff that would affect 40 percent of the company's employees, and Carol Ann only had three more months before she too would be laid off. Carol Ann was a recruiter.

Now she'd have to give up her dream of being a generalist and look for another recruiter position, if she could find one in a down job market.

Carol Ann went to Donna for help. Even though giving Carol Ann the generalist position she was looking for was now impossible, Donna was determined to do what she could to help Carol Ann pursue her goal. There must be something Donna could say yes to.

This is the three-month plan they came up with. First, Carol Ann would apprentice herself to the benefits department, so that she could learn how to give the basic benefits presentation to the people who were laid off. The benefits people were grateful for the help.

Next, she used her recruitment experience to develop two workshops for people who had lost their jobs. She asked for feedback on her workshop and on her presentation skills from a trainer who was laid off. The trainer was happy to help.

Little by little, with Donna's encouragement, Carol Ann acquired some of the basics of all the human resources specialties and had references from people in each one. At the end of three months, Carol Ann was exhausted, but happy. She had the experience to present herself as a generalist. She got the first generalist job she applied for. Donna was proud of what she had done to make it possible.

If you can say yes to something, you can satisfy many people. You'll also develop an excellent personal reputation that will serve you for your entire career.

Pay Attention to How You Are Feeling

Your own feelings can affect your responses to people asking you for something. This can be especially true when what they are asking for is something you believe you were owed, but never received. Then, when you respond to what is being asked of you, the feelings can dominate your response.

This is a particular problem for people who are what we call natural managers—people who are excellent at managing their own staff, when they themselves aren't being managed in the same way. They say things like:

"Nobody helps me with my career; why should I be helping her?"

Or

"Why should I let him leave an hour early to take that class when I can't even budget a class for myself?"

Or

"Why should I let her take three weeks' vacation together when I had to take a beeper with me on my last vacation and even came in to the office once or twice?"

When you find yourself thinking that way, take a minute before you answer the person making the request. Are you feeling angry or resentful? If you are, you are probably not evaluating the request in a reasonable way. You are likely to be more negative than you should be.

On the other hand, just because you are offering someone an opportunity you haven't had doesn't mean you should always say yes and suffer in silence. Being a great manager does not mean being a martyr. Martyrs make terrible role models in organizations.

If you are feeling this resentment, it might mean that you need to work on your skills for managing your own manager. Whom do you know and respect who does a great job of managing bosses and who would be willing to help you improve this skill? Finding an informal coach is an excellent way to improve skills.

What else could you do to have more of an influence in your organization, to get more of what you need to be happy and successful at work? It's pretty common for managers, particularly first line managers, to neglect their own needs in favor of the company's needs or their staff's needs. But remember that you are a role model for the people who work for you. People will imitate what you do. It's important for you to show them that it is possible to be happy and successful at work. The answer may very well be for you to go back to the first section of this book, identify what you need, and ask for it.

Be the Person You Want to Be

We all live within our own comfort zones. Inside the zone, everything is predictable and comfortable. We may not be happy or satisfied. We may not be the people we want to be, but we feel safe. The comfort zone might be a geographic one— "I feel comfortable working in Chicago, but I'd never want to work in L.A." It might be a professional one—"I'm really a database programmer." Or, it might be associated with a particular employer— "I've been at GM (or Merck, or Kaiser Permanente, or the University of Missouri), for fifteen years now. I can't see myself anywhere else." Or, it might be a skill or behavior that seems out of reach—"I'd never be able to make a presentation in front of a hundred people." Or, "I'm not the kind of person who feels comfortable asking for a new assignment."

That's a perfectly reasonable way to live your work life—unless your personal comfort zone is too small for you, that is. Or, if you don't feel you can be the person you want to be and still stay inside your comfort zone.

Think for a minute about the people you know who have huge comfort zones. They seem less afraid of trying new things. They seem to have more contacts and connections. They seem to have more and broader experiences. More opportunities come to them—not just for jobs, but even for professions and assignments. What would it take to be like them?

The easy way to expand your comfort zone is to ask for what you need to be happy and satisfied at work. Yes, that's a moving target. At different times in your life, you will want a different balance between your work life and your personal life. Or you may be inspired to try out something new. No matter how committed you are to your current job, sooner or later you will want to expand your knowledge and skills. All these changes in your interests and your needs will stretch your idea of the person you want to be.

Every time you change your idea of what you want to be, you will be in the position of asking again. As you grow and as your comfort zone grows, you will think of new things you want and need. Every time you ask for what you need, you decrease the distance between the person you are and the person you want to be.

The first time you use what you have learned here, ask for something easy to ask for. Follow the steps outlined in this book:

- Know what you need and prepare your request

- Think through the possible answers you will get and how you will respond

- Identify all the possible people who could help you get what you need

- Turn the tables and consider what would happen if you were the person being asked

These steps won't guarantee you will get what you ask for, but they will make it more likely.

Don't push yourself too much. If you try for something that is too difficult or frightening, you may never ask again. If you wanted to learn public speaking, for example, it would be a mistake to start with a complex presentation in front of a critical audience. The experience could be such a harrowing one that you avoid public speaking in the future, no matter how well received the presentation actually was. Start with something that is just within the range of comfort for you, and build on that success.

To borrow an image and a concept from William Sloane Coffin Jr., you can be the person you want to be without ever leaving your comfort zone. All that is necessary is that you move to the edge of your comfort zone, and stand there.

Soon, you will find that the place where you are standing has become a part of your comfort zone. Then, move to the edge of your comfort zone again, and stand there. In that way, you can comfortably expand what you do. You can become the person you want to become. You can make the contribution you want to make.

Once you have established a pattern of asking for what you want and need at work, you will become more practiced at knowing when and how and whom to ask. You will see opportunities you hadn't known were there. Your view of who you are and what you can become will grow, just as Eva's did.

Eva:

Eva's parents were killed in a tragic automobile accident when she was in her second year of college. Even though she managed to finish out the year, thanks to her part-time clerical job, Eva wasn't in the mood to go back to college, and she didn't have the money to anyway. So she asked her boss at her part-time job if she knew of any full-time administrative jobs that were open. Eva was a bright, energetic person, so her boss referred her to a friend who was starting his own business.

As secretary to an entrepreneur, Eva found herself doing a little bit of everything—finding office space, buying furniture, helping the accounting firm set up the books, helping the computer consultant set up the computers, and helping the insurance firm set up the insurance and benefits for the five people who had been hired. She was very busy and learning a lot. As the company grew, Eva's job grew from being the official meet-and-greeter for new hires, to placing the ads and screening candidates.

She asked for the opportunity, and the entrepreneur was happy to have the help.

Eva noticed that the people she interviewed were telling her that the benefit package was not up to what other companies were offering. She asked the insurance agent if he thought that was true. He suggested that she survey competitors and find out. Eva did some research and found a local professional association of compensation and benefits people. She asked for permission to join the group, but was only given the authorization to attend three meetings. But that didn't stop Eva.

On her own, she analyzed the benefits package her company offered. The candidates were right; the package wasn't competitive. One of her colleagues in the professional association got her started, and her company's accounting firm helped her cost out the new proposal. Then, she made a presentation to her company's senior management of a new benefits package that would cost the same as the old one, but offer much more to the employees.

The presentation was a huge success, and Eva followed up by asking for the position of human resources manager. She had the backing of everybody—from the people she had hired, to the insurance agent, the accounting firm, and the colleagues she met in the professional association.

Since then, Eva has used her skill at asking to move to a larger company, to complete her BA and acquire an executive MBA, to have a stint as a consultant, to try out a sales career, and to move to a career in banking. She now runs a major retail division of a large regional bank.

"I guess you could say that I'm one of those people who has had a really great career by asking people for their help. Most of the time people were more than willing to help me. I've gone places and done things I never imagined I would. For the most part, I've been very happy in my jobs. People tell me I've been very lucky, but a lot of the time I've asked for that luck."